spiritual realities

Volume 6

THE NATURE
OF CREATION

by
Harold R. Eberle

Winepress Publishing
Yakima, Washington, USA

Spiritual Realities, Volume VI:
The Nature of Creation

© 2000 by Harold R. Eberle

Winepress Publishing
P.O. Box 10653
Yakima, WA 98909-1653
509-248-5837

Library of Congress Control No. 00-132997
ISBN 1-882523-17-2

Cover by Jeff Boettcher

Unless otherwise stated, all biblical quotations are taken from the *New American Standard Bible* © 1977, The Lockman Foundation, La Habra, California 90631.

Printed in the United States of America

Thanks and Dedication

Several science teachers and enthusiasts read the manuscript of this book, giving their suggestions and advice which is greatly appreciated. Special thanks should be given to Nelson Martin who picked through it word by word while we were ministering in Africa together. Edward McIsaac added insights without which the arguments of this book would have seemed weak. James Bryson is a newly discovered treasure who can edit and improve my most complicated sentences. Also, I had input and editing advice from Peter Eisenmann, Brian Stevens, and Dennis Jacobson. Each of these has left his mark on these pages, but Annette Bradley is the one in whom I put my trust for her scrutinizing work before sending the final product to the printing press.

This book is dedicated to our youngest son, Peter David Eberle, who has a zest for life which surely will keep me young for years to come. He is also one of the most giving and observant people I ever have known.

Table Of Contents

Introduction

Throughout history people have accredited to God, gods, or the supernatural realm that which they cannot understand. Primitive tribes explain rain and thunder as the activities of divine beings. The illusionist deceives his spectators into believing that real magic is at work. Stars once were considered supreme beings. Even early scientists thought the earth was flat and supported by god-like creatures. All unexplained phenomena were accredited to the invisible world.

As science progressed, one belief after another moved from supernatural to natural understanding. However, science never has taken mankind deeper than the point of contact with God. His point of contact with nature is where science always has stopped and always will.

This volume identifies that point of contact which God has with our created world. It tackles some of the big questions concerning how science and the Bible complement each other. It puts into a biblical framework society's progress, technology, evolution, death, our expanding universe, natural laws, life on other planets, time, and quantum mechanics.

Let's take a brave look at our universe through biblically trained eyes.

God's Resonating Glory

When God spoke into existence the light, stars, earth, animals, plants—all of creation—He released His own nature. Like an artist reveals himself in his work, so also God left His imprint upon all He made. We can study creation as if it were God's self-portrait.

Who is God? Romans 1:20 tells us:

> *For since the creation of the world His invisible attributes, His eternal power and divine nature, have been clearly seen, being understood, through what has been made....*

God's eternal power and divine nature can be seen in the stars, the oceans, and the mountains. His invisible attributes are evident in the clouds above, the air around us, and the ground beneath us. Who He is—this is being declared every minute of every day by all of creation.*

---

* Note that we neither are giving credence to worshipping creation nor treating it as if it were God. We simply are acknowledging how God reveals Himself in His creation

Envision the outgoing power of God's spoken Word. As a tuning fork can be struck and continues to resonate, so also when God spoke things into existence He released His glory from out of His own nature—that glory continues resonating today.

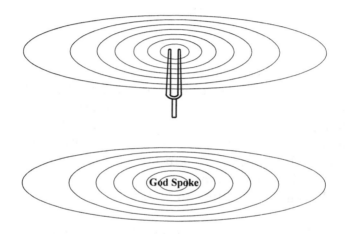

God Spoke

When we hear the sound of an instrument we recognize the instrument that made it. Similarly, as we behold the glory of creation, we can sense the nature of its Source, that is, the nature of God.

As astronomers explore the galaxies and find no outer boundaries to our expanding universe, they are beholding the immensity of God. As biologists study the nature of living things, they are investigating the nature of Him who released life into this world. As you gaze upon a flower, a bird, or an insect, you are seeing the wonders of the God who is in the smallest detail.

As man studies the world around him, it is possible for him not only to learn scientific facts, but also to *experience the glory* of creation.

In Spiritual Realities Volume V, we explained how the spirit of man can "harmonize" with his surroundings. When two tuning forks of similar frequency are brought together and one is struck, the second will also begin vibrating. In similar fashion, if you sit in a forest and quiet yourself for an extended period, you can sense the glory of God still resonating there. You can *come into harmony* with your surroundings and experience the nature of God who created all things.

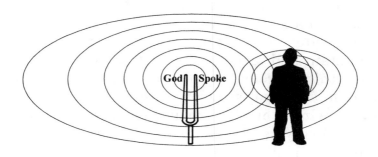

There are different aspects of God's glory which can be experienced. The apostle Paul explained:

> *There is one glory of the sun, and another glory of the moon, and another glory of the stars; for star differs from star in glory.* (I Cor. 15:41)

In the same context, Paul talked about the various forms of life, saying:

> *All flesh is not the same flesh, but there is one flesh of men, and another flesh of beasts, and another flesh of birds, and another of fish.*
>
> (I Cor. 15:39)

Each and every created thing bears the wonderful imprint of God's glory in a unique fashion.

Because man has the ability to experience various glories, he can sense the changes as he exposes himself to different aspects of creation. For example, a person can sit in front of an aquarium and watch the fish; in time he may be drawn in and overwhelmed by the beauty of the underwater world. Or a person can climb a mountain and feel the size and magnificence of everything around him. An astronomer can search for solar systems beyond ours and be overwhelmed by the expanse of everything out there. Every aspect of creation may be observed, studied, and discovered; and the glory of God can be experienced.

Picture the days of creation like a symphony with every sound bursting forth. Each time God spoke He released new sound—incredible beauty. The tones released in the beginning continue through time. As a cymbal—once hit—continues vibrating and sending forth its tone, so also, all of creation is resonating from the Voice which spoke in the beginning.

The Force of Progress

To see God's glory in creation, we should look closer at His highest work—man. Mankind actually was created in God's image. Not only did God release an aspect of His nature into man, but He actually patterned man after Himself. We are fearfully and wonderfully made (Ps. 139:14). After God completed His work of creation, the Bible tells us that He called it "very good" (Gen. 1:31). This included mankind, hence we know that man also was created "very good."

God did not stop there. He *blessed* mankind. As we have been teaching, there is a measure of God's nature, power, and glory released every time He speaks. Genesis 1:28 says:

> *And God blessed them; and God said to them, "Be fruitful and multiply, and fill the earth, and subdue it...."*

This was more than a commission or a command; it was a *blessing*. With God's blessing, power is released. This power released a force which moves people in a positive direction.

Understanding this *force* is central to understanding man. In every human being there is a force compelling him or her to fill and subdue the earth. This force drives people to get out of bed, build homes, and go to work. Because of this force, mankind builds roads, plants crops, and moves mountains. It is the force of progress.

This force exists within each one of us. Therefore, it is frustrating for a person who does not get ahead and has to struggle with the same difficulties year after year. People get bored doing the same activities, wearing the same style of clothes, and not advancing beyond the position of the generation before them. This force is part of our nature.

This same force is evident in society as a whole. Every generation builds on the knowledge, labor, and experience of the preceding generations. Cities are constructed, forms of transportation are improved, technology is advanced. Society is moving in a direction, and that direction is advancement toward the goal of filling and subduing the earth. This is progress.

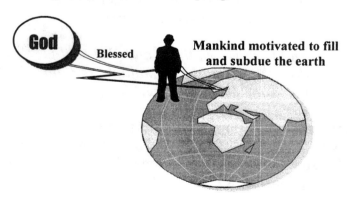

God's first blessing released a *force of progress* which has been active throughout all of history and still is active today. Just as God's Words, *"Let the earth bring forth vegetation,"* released a force which causes plants to go on reproducing throughout the duration of this world, so also God's Words over Adam and Eve activated a force pushing mankind to act continually in the direction of filling the earth and taking dominion.*

Notice that the force of God's first blessing includes sexual drives, hunger, and ambition. When we break this force of blessing into these categories, we are not giving credence to evil desires nor of man submitting to over-indulgences. No. We acknowledge that man can become controlled and at times overtaken by these forces to such an extent that he falls out of God's will and into sin. However, what we are identifying here is that there is a real force, originally released by God, which causes mankind to progress.

Envision this force as a wave originating at the beginning and moving forward through time. Riding the crest of this wave are pioneers, inventors, innovators, and researchers. At the front of the wave are those who advance society: political leaders pointing the way; songwriters expressing the hearts of people; authors writing books; artists catching the wind and pointing people

---

* We do not use the term *dominion* in the negative sense of control or domination, but rather, being a steward of, caring for, managing and tending.

down specific paths. Think of those people who are driven from within to explore new territories, engineer technological advancements, and discover medical breakthroughs. What motivates these people, often at great personal sacrifice? It is the force of God's spoken Words at creation. It is the very blessing of God made manifest.

Think of a new idea which you once had, perhaps to start a business or invent something which would improve life. Did you ever notice that if you fail to carry out that idea, someone else often comes up with a similar idea? Why does this happen? Because society is moving in a direction and each step is unfolding in a progressive manner.

Yes, there is a wind, a wave, a force pushing all of society toward the filling of this earth, taking dominion over one challenge after another.

This has tremendous implications for our future. Since the world is moving in the direction of progress, will we:

> Conquer all diseases?
> Master every corner of this earth?
> Provide a home for every person?
> Grow trees exactly where we choose?
> Decide where every animal will roam?
> Genetically engineer human beings without deformity?
> Eventually have unlimited energy?
> Form one-world government with peace reigning?

Provide food for every human?
Create a utopia?

No, we will not. However, that is the *direction* in which mankind is motivated. Yet because of sin, we shall fail.

The Opposing Force of Sin

God released a power into the world to propel mankind ahead, but there also exists a curse due to sin. If Adam and Eve (nor any other human being) had not sinned, we eventually would have filled the whole earth and created a utopia for all. Yet because of sin, we are frustrated in this goal, "weeds are growing in our garden," and new obstacles constantly are appearing before us.

Jesus explained that the world is like a farmer's field in which good seeds were sown, but an enemy also sowed bad seeds (Matt. 13:24-30). In time, both good and bad seeds sprouted. The workers asked the farmer if they should pull up the bad plants, but he answered, "No, lest you pull up the good with the bad." Our Lord explained that on the last day a harvest will take place in which the good and bad will be separated.

This is how we should view the world as it advances throughout history and on into the future. The world is like a farm. Things are growing, they are progressing, they are moving in a positive direction. However, negative factors also are appearing and growing. Mankind will not conquer evil through his own ingenuity or creativity, though he is motivated to try all the days of his life. Ultimately, it will take the intervention of God to bring final order, justice, freedom, and abundance to this earth.

Recognize two forces—or energies—at work: the force of progress and the power of sin.

Some Christian groups emphasize only one of these forces at work in the world. Those who see only the power to progress, wrongly think we someday will arrive at utopia on this earth. They deny the ongoing effects of sin.

Other Christian groups only recognize the power of sin. They envision a world getting worse every day. They wrongly think that life was perfect in the beginning and that society is decaying morally, spiritually, and hence, in every way. They view things only from a declining perspective.

This declining view is fixed so firmly in some Christians' minds that they have to be radically challenged before they will embrace the truth. The truth is that society was neither morally nor spiritually superior in the first generations of man. The Bible shows us that Adam and Eve's own son, Cain, murdered his brother, Abel. To put things in perspective, we can point out that at the beginning of civilization, 100% of the families on the earth had a murderer in their midst. In contrast, we can point out that 100% of today's families do not have an actual murderer among them. Of course, we all experience anger and hate, but rarely to the point of actually murdering a family member.

Further, we can point out that in Noah's time the world became so evil that God saw it necessary to destroy humanity. When God looked at man He saw "...that every intent of the thoughts of his heart was only evil continually" (Gen. 6:5). Of course, there is evil in the world today, but God has not decided to destroy us, and we cannot say that every person's thoughts are evil continually. I have some good thoughts. Don't you?

The truth is that we are *not* living in the most evil generation. Throughout history there have been people who have risen in holiness, while others have declined. This is very evident in the Old Testament as the Jewish people followed various leaders, some who were righteous and others who were evil. So too throughout history we can see that society changes both positively and negatively.

More importantly, we need to realize that *there is no ruling force causing mankind to decline morally year by year.* Yes, sin is in the world because of Adam; yes, sin opposes us; yes, it impedes our progress. However, we have a freewill, and hence, we can improve or backslide morally. We have *not* been sentenced to a downhill slide because of sin.

Furthermore, it would be biblically inaccurate for us to think that Adam was intellectually superior to all his descendants. Sometime Christians exaggerate Adam's intellectual ability, arguing that he was able to name all of the animals which God created. That, however, is wrong. Adam did *not* name all of the animals. What the Bible tells us is that he "...gave names to all the cattle, and to the birds of the sky, and to every beast of the field..." (Gen. 2:20). Adam did not name the fish, nor the amphibians, nor the reptiles, nor the swimming mammals, nor the rodents, nor the insects, nor the bacteria, nor the vast majority of creatures on the earth.

To convince you that naming the cattle, birds, and beasts of the field was no great intellectual feat, allow me to mention my own personal experience in this area. Before going into the ministry, I worked in the field of wildlife management. While I was earning my university degree, it only took one quarter for me and my fellow students to learn the names of every bird in our region of the world. It took a similar length of time to learn the scientific (in Latin) and common names of the mammals and fish. In addition, we had to memorize hundreds of facts about all of these animals. We would have been delighted and greatly relieved only to have been required to learn the names of the cattle, birds, and beasts of the field.

To say that Adam was so superior to man today is to blow out of proportion what the Bible tells us that he actually did.

Of course, Adam was morally innocent before he sinned; however, intellectually he did not know how to build an airplane nor a computer. Among Cain's descendants, we are told that Enoch built a city, Jubal was the father of those who played certain musical instruments, and Tubal-cain was the forger of tools made of bronze and iron (Gen. 4:17-22). Society does progress! God created people with the ability to learn. Information is passed from generation to generation in a cumulative fashion.

The Genesis society was not perfect. There was evil and ignorance to overcome, just as in today's society.

It is wrong to think of society merely as declining or advancing. We have identified two major forces at work in mankind: the force of sin and the force of God's blessing to progress. We should also consider the added blessings released when people repent and turn to God—He responds with further blessings.

In the future, mankind will continue on a course toward dominion, yet obstacles will continue to appear. We constantly will discover new medicines, but new diseases will arise. Technology and engineering advancements will make life easier year by year, yet new challenges always will stand before us. Through advancements in farming techniques, we will learn how to provide enough food for the whole world, yet the poor we always will have with us (John 12:8). Governmental systems will progress until mankind literally ends all war and enforces one-world government, yet people always will fight with one another.

Of course, we only will advance until the Lord appears and brings an end to the present system. If He delays long, the force of progress will take us to places of dominion which today we cannot comprehend. Even now we are reaching a state of people working together worldwide never before seen in human history. Compare this with how people worked together at the time of the Tower of Babel. God said:

> *"Behold, they are one people, and they all have the same language. And this is what they began to do, and now nothing which they purpose to do will be impossible for them."* (Gen. 11:6)

Notice what God said: He acknowledged that mankind—working together—could accomplish whatever they purposed to do.

Of course, God confused the people's language at that point, but today we are approaching similar conditions. Present forms of communication and computer technology are uniting us, creating the availability of knowledge, thoughts, desires, and goals to all people. The implications of this are profound. God said that nothing shall be impossible for mankind if they purpose together as one.

God can "confuse the languages" and intervene at any point He chooses. However, what we hope you see is the *direction* in which this world is moving. Furthermore, that progress toward dominion is *accelerating*.

As a final note on this subject, we point out that the force of progress is good. It originated with God for the benefit of man. Some Christians have a negative attitude toward progress, technology, and, generally speaking, toward anything new. This is wrong. The basic force which pushes mankind was instilled in us by God. Of course, men can use the force to further evil ends, however, we must realize that the advancement of society toward filling and subduing the earth was in God's plan from the beginning.

Forces of Life and Disorganization

In the previous chapter, we discussed two opposing forces working on mankind: the force of progress and the force of sin. Now we can identify two corresponding forces at work on the whole of creation.

First, let's identify the *force of life* which pushes living things to move in the direction of becoming more and more organized. Single-celled organisms multiply; cells grow into thousands, each with complex functions of life. A bird egg develops and hatches to release a bird. A mammal grows to maturity, increasing in size by organizing millions of chemicals into the building blocks of life. Animals build homes, gather food, and organize the world around themselves in ways beneficial to their own survival. Life moves in the positive direction of organization.

This *push of life* entails more than just increased organization. It also causes seeds to sprout, roots to push into the soil, and plants to reach toward heaven. It is the power which motivates animals continually to search for food, to reproduce, and to survive.

THE FORCE OR PUSH OF LIFE

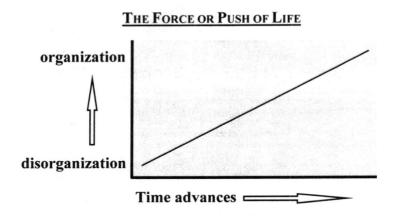

Life is busy. It crawls into every space: worms live in glaciers, trees cling to small crevices in mountains, birds soar through the sky, and fish search the ocean floors. There is a push of life which causes all living things to keep moving ahead. This force underlies and permeates every living thing.

We are not talking about evolution here. Different readers have different views on evolution, and I will address that topic in the next chapter. Here we simply are speaking of the all-pervasive *push of life*. Why do plants grow? Why do animals seek to survive? What is the motivating force behind life?

Labeling this force "the struggle to survive" or similar names does not explain where it originated. Obviously, life would not continue if a survival force did not exist or even if it diminished much in strength. However, recognizing that it exists does not tell us where or how it originated.

Compare the survival of living things with a race in which many automobiles are speeding ahead. The fastest and most reliable cars will reach the finish line first. However, recognizing this fact does not explain what is driving the cars ahead. In the exact same way, we can recognize a force driving plants and animals to reproduce and extend their existence to the next generation; however, that does not tell us from where that force comes.

Every thinking person, Christian and non-Christian, must admit that this force is real and that life could not go on even a day without it. Yet science can offer no explanation for the origin of this force which permeates all of life.

The Bible tells us. In the beginning God said:

> *"Let the earth sprout vegetation, plants yielding seed, and fruit trees bearing fruit....Let the waters teem with swarms of living creatures, and let birds fly above the earth....Let the earth bring forth living creatures after their kind...."*
>
> (Gen. 1:11-24)

Consider the power in God's spoken Words. See His Words not only as powerful enough to start life, but actually to sustain it and drive it ahead.

In Volume IV of this Spiritual Realities series, we studied how words spoken in faith proceed from the speaker until they accomplish that which they were sent out to do. God created the world by His spoken Word. Isaiah tells us that God's Words never return void but continue producing until everything for which they have been sent out is accomplished (Is. 55:11). God's Words spoken at creation not only started living things, but released a force which continues even today. That is, the push of life.

Science can study it but cannot explain it. Science can measure how fast a plant grows but cannot tell us why it grows. Science may discover chemicals which increase, retard, or even stop growth, but it does not explain why plants even possess the ability to grow. Science can observe a force pushing every living thing, but it cannot tell us from where this push comes

The Bible gives us a Source. God said, *"Let the earth bring forth...."* His Word advances and sustains all of life.

Having identified this force which moves living things in the direction of increased organization, we now can look at the opposing force.

Scientists say that everything is increasing in *entropy*. By this they mean that all things become more and more random and chaotic as time progresses. In addition, they move toward their lowest state of energy. This is referred to as *The Second Law of Thermodynamics*. Isaac Newton (1796-1832) and other scientists studied and defined it for us. Today, scientists accept this as a fundamental Law which governs the whole of the universe.

In layman's terms, things are falling apart. Complex structures gradually break down. If metal is left unattended it will rust away. Stars burn out of existence after years and years. Everything that has been created is moving in the direction of less organization.

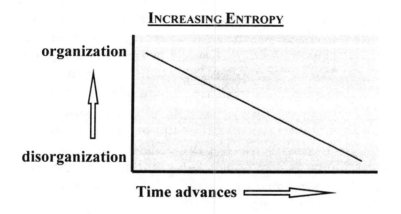

We must not think of this force as entirely negative, for the world as we know it could not exist without it. Every chemical reaction is dependent upon the forces which push them to their lowest state of energy. Plants could not live, heat would not move from one place to another, and even the sun would not shine if the Second Law of Thermodynamics was not governing the universe. Therefore, we must realize that this is a good Law which God imposed over His creation.

However, there is a negative element in this Second Law of Thermodynamics. It would be nice if some things did not rust, rot, or burn up. Everything you build will someday fall apart.

Living things must fight against this force and often they are overcome by it to the extent that they die. Indeed, every living things is overcome in time. This uncontrollable force of increasing disorganization acts on things in ways which we do not always desire.

The Bible explains how, since the fall of Adam and Eve, the earth does not respond completely as man desires. The Scriptures refer to "...the ground which the Lord has cursed" (Gen. 5:29). When God spoke, "Cursed is the ground," it began to produce thorns and thistles (Gen. 3:17-18). Since that day it has required mankind extra work, even by the sweat of his brow, to make the earth produce what he wants it to produce.

There is a negative element not just in the earth, but encompassing all of creation. The apostle Paul explains to us:

> *For the creation was subjected to futility, not of its own will, but because of Him who subjected it, in hope that the creation itself also will be set free from its slavery to corruption....* (Rom. 8:20-21)

Notice that God placed upon all creation a force that enslaves it to corruption. It has been subjected to futility.

It is unclear from Scripture exactly what this curse entails. Perhaps God accelerated the forces of increasing entropy. Maybe He merely sentenced all things to end in futility. Or perhaps man's relationship to the universe changed in that he now tends to fight the forces of corruption.

Though we do not understand this curse fully, we can point out that it works contrary to the force of life. It is not the Second Law of Thermodynamics, but there is inherent within this Law a negative element. This curse is more than a force which results in living things dying, but in some way it enslaves creation. It pushes against it. It imprisons it.

When we read the context of the passage in Romans, chapter eight, we learn that this force of corruption someday will be ended when God intervenes. Indeed, it is only the injection of His life which can overcome this element of corruption resulting from the curse.

We have identified two forces governing the created universe: the force of life and the force of increasing entropy. In addition, we are recognizing the negative element of corruption.

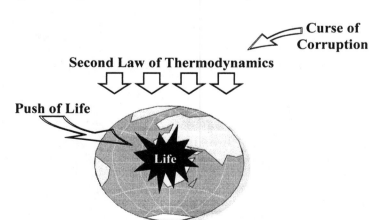

27

Finally, notice that the push of life overcomes the force of increasing entropy. Living things organize millions of molecules into unique and intricate patterns necessary for building, growth, energy, and reproduction. As long as plants, animals, and humans are alive, they overcome the negative forces working against them. However, when death comes, the force of life ceases. The force of increasing entropy overcomes, and the process of disorganization wins out. As we know, even man returns to dust.

The Origin of Life

Having identified the *force of life* which propels all living things in a positive direction, it is time we address the topic of evolution versus creationism. The theory of evolution teaches that all of life evolved over the course of millions of years from simple, non-living compounds into more and more complex life forms. On the other hand, Creationism refers to the belief that God created life during a six-day period just a few thousand years ago as is literally recorded in the Bible. There are many people who combine these two views or modify them to fit their own understanding, but here I will use these terms to refer to the two positions just defined.

I know in addressing this issue that I am risking the loss and anger of many of my readers since Christians are divided over the related issues, and many have strong feelings on each side. With hopes of gaining your ears, allow me to mention my credentials from a secular viewpoint. While earning a Bachelor of Science degree in related fields, I was fully indoctrinated into the views of evolutionary theory. However, during that period I spent extensive time studying the arguments and scientific evidence put forth by creationists. I am fully aware of the arguments for a young earth including those related to uranium and strontium thorium decay, mineral deposits in our oceans, cosmic dust buildup, radiocarbon dating, decay of our magnetic fields, and other methods. I am aware of the missing links in the fossil record and some of the mathematical improbabilities involved with the theory of evolution. From those and other studies, I became knowledgeable enough on the related subjects so that I spoke more than once at secular universities, addressing students of biology and medicine. I mention these qualifications to reassure you that I understand both sides of the arguments thoroughly.

Years ago I became known as a strong, public advocate of the creationist view; however, I can no longer embrace *some* of the views taught by the most known creationists who write and speak in the Christian community on these subjects today. Please do not jump to conclusions—I do not accept the complete theory of evolution as held by many secular scientists—I believe God created all things as recorded in the book of Genesis. However, I have come to see that many of the traditional creationists interpret key Bible passages in a way with which I can no longer agree. In addition, there are some concepts which the evolutionary scientists teach, which now I do accept as true.

As I explain the transition that has taken place in my own thinking over the last few years, keep in mind the strict creationist viewpoint from which I have come. Some of my traditional creationist friends may think I am losing a foothold in truths they hold dear. At the other extreme are Christian brothers and sisters who believe in the theory of evolution, and perhaps years ago they came to some of the conclusions which I will explain in the next few pages. All I can share with you is the process of change that has occurred in my own life and share honestly how I see things today.

To begin, let me state that there is a God-instilled force in plants and animals that causes them to advance. If you followed the discussion in the preceding chapters, you will have seen this. In chapter two we discussed the power of God's spoken Word which causes mankind to progress. In chapter four we explained the push of life which causes living organisms to organize the elements of this world in a positive fashion. These are real powers finding their source in God's spoken Word.

Now we ask the question, "Did God's spoken Word release enough power to cause living things to change and adapt to their environment?" We accept the fact that the push of life causes plants and animals to reproduce and struggle to survive. But is that push of life great enough to cause living things to adapt to their environment? And then we should ask, "Can those changes be passed from generation to generation?"

With these questions in mind, consider first the human race. Both evolutionists and creationists believe that all mankind has one common ancestor. Creationists believe, as I do, that ancestor to be Adam. Acts 17:26 tells us:

> ...and He [God] made from one, every nation of mankind to live on all the face of the earth....

Though we have one forefather, we can see many different features, colors, sizes, and shapes among the human race. Traditional creationists explain this variety by saying Adam was created perfect and must have had within his genetic code the variety necessary to produce the different races of people. That explanation, however, is inadequate. If we take the Bible literally we must recognize that Noah and his three sons were also the forefathers of the human race. Therefore, the traditional creationist must also believe that Noah, his sons and daughters-in-law had all the genetic information within them to produce the variety we see in the human race today.

Of course, that is possible, because anything is possible with God. However, it seems to me much more reasonable to think that God instilled in the nature of man (and all living things) the ability to change, adapt, and advance. We are not talking about random mutation and natural selection—for there is *no real positive force—no push of life*—in the secular understanding of evolution. We are saying that God has instilled a positive force in life by the power of His spoken Word—hence, we have such variety in the present human race.

This issue really comes down to our understanding of God's spoken Word. Does His Word proceed from His mouth and *continue producing* whatever it is sent out to do? The answer is, "Yes" (Is. 55:11). His Word has creative power inherent within it. Even after God released His Words, those Words *continued creating.*

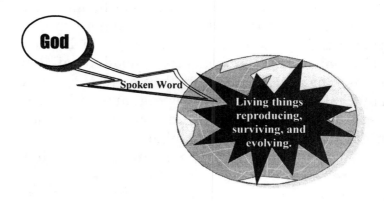

This ongoing, creative force has been released into all plants and animals. Therefore, it is reasonable and logical to say that God released into living things the ability to adapt to their environment. As those changes happen within the reproductive genes, those adaptations will be passed from one generation to another. This is evolution. It is not evolution dependent merely on chance mutation and natural selection, however, it is evolution.

Some of my strict creationist friends will think I am crumbling from the faith by accepting any form of evolution. Let me reassure them that I continue to believe that man did *not evolve* from lower forms of life and is in fact a *distinct and unique creation of God.* Furthermore, the Bible tells us that *God created plants and animals as distinct kinds.* I do not accept the evolutionary views which attempt to explain life without God. In fact, the idea that chance mutation and natural selection (Darwin's explanation) can account for the intricacies of life is so mathematically improbable that it is ridiculous. I am not going to repeat the mathematical arguments which some creationists have so wonderfully made available to us; however, I simply will refer to them and say that the view which sees organized life coming forth from disorganization merely by chance mutation is absurdly impossible.

However, I have come to understand that God released a *positive (creative) force* in all of life. Mutation and natural selection cannot explain evolution, but the Bible reveals to us a force which God released into the plant and animal world. That force does cause living things to advance. It is not mutation and natural selection which causes living things to advance, but God's spoken Word. In light of this, I dare say that Christians, more than anyone else, should believe plants and animals evolve. We have discovered the Source for positive advancement.

I am not saying we should accept the whole theory of evolution which claims that higher forms of life evolved from lower forms of life. However, to believe that animals genetically change, adapt, and pass positive characteristics to succeeding generations is in accordance with our biblical understanding of how God created things. Plants and animals do evolve (adapting to their environment and passing those changes on to later generations), because God's spoken Word continues producing what it is sent out to do.

It is interesting that many traditional creationists believe animals evolve in an entirely different manner. They think God created plants and animals "good" in the sense of no imperfections nor subjection to disease, enemies, or death. They envision the fall of Adam bringing a curse of death upon all living things. As a consequence, they see death and weaknesses existing only after Adam's sin but not before. In the next chapter I will show why this is an unbiblical view, but here I want to show the contradiction within the traditional creationist's own mind. Most creationists envision animals killing each other only after the fall of mankind, hence, wild animals growing sharper teeth, some bacteria becoming parasitic (in a sense, evil), and all living things developing defenses against one another. Creationists typically ignore the fact that to believe such changes have come upon the plant and animal kingdom since the fall (in the last 6000 years) is to believe in more dramatic evolution (that is, change which can be passed on genetically) than even the secular evolutionists teach.

Pointing this fact out to traditional creationists often shocks them, because they never have recognized how dramatic a form of genetic change, that is, "evolution," they believe.

I give place for more than "microevolution," which entails only minor changes within species. Plants and animals evolve on a larger scale. The traditional creationist will admit that dogs can be bred over several generations with certain characteristics selected and enhanced: this is microevolution. However, God has instilled within the nature of life the ability to evolve beyond that level.

In the creation account recorded in chapter one of Genesis, we read that God blessed the plant and animal kingdoms in order that they would reproduce after their "own kind" (Gen. 1:21, 24-25). Traditional creationists take this terminology to mean that one species can only reproduce offspring of its own species. For example, even though dogs may be bred to enhance certain characteristics, they will always be dogs. One species is never changed to another species in the traditional creationist's view.

I do not believe the biblical term "kind" puts such limits on reproduction. To take a biblical term like "kind" and equate it with our modern scientific term "species" is wrong. In fact, in the creation account as recorded in Genesis, God tells us the meaning of the word "kind." In the same verses that use "kind," we are told that He created the swarms of living creatures, the birds, the sea creatures, cattle, creeping things, and beasts (Gen. 1:20-24). Species terminology is not used. To impose our scientific definition of species is wrong. If we are to accept the Genesis categories of animal life, we would have to say that birds produce birds, fish produce fish, insects produce insects, etc. However, to say that one bird cannot evolve into another species of birds is to add to what the Bible teaches. It simply is not in the Word of God.

Therefore, I am stating that animals may evolve within their own kind.

Indeed, I would go further and declare that evolution within "kinds" is a wonderful feature instilled by God in the very nature of living things. God *"blessed"* them (Gen. 1:22), that is He released a *positive (creative) force* within the nature of living things to cause them to advance. In a similar fashion to how He blessed mankind to progress, so God blessed the plant and animal kingdom. There is a force within causing living things to survive, adapt, and even evolve in positive ways.

Therefore, Bible-believing Christians should not be totally condemning of the idea that plants and animals evolve. Obviously, we cannot accept the whole theory of evolution which attempts to explain life without God. However, we can agree and even commend biologists who have discovered a force in life which causes plants and animals to advance. The tragedy would be for us to react so negatively to their discovery that we completely abandon them in their pursuit of truth. Instead, Christians should be involved, contributing a biblical perspective to the discovery of the force of life.

What then is the origin of life? God created all things. He created plants and animals in distinct categories as recorded in the book of Genesis. However, if a group of plants or animals become separated, such as living on an island separate from others of their own species, they may evolve to fit that new environment. Even in the midst of a plant or animal population, positive new characteristics may appear in order to help God's creatures survive. Not only is this biblical, but is also supported by present fossil records and other scientific evidence.

Anyone with a knowledge of the present fossil record would agree that animals do appear in the record in distinct categories, that is, kinds. There have been a handful of fossils proposed as "evolutionary links" or "transitional types" between kinds; however, every honest scientist—evolutionist or creationist—has to admit that the proposed links are few and far between. Furthermore, if the theory of evolution were true, transitional fossils would be abundant in the fossil record. This is true, because it would take the greatest periods of time and transitional steps (millions in some cases) for animals to make these transitions. Instead, we find millions of fossils which fit into a category of kind, while there are little to no fossils which can be labeled transitional types.

To summarize, God created the world just as recorded it in the Bible. Because God's Words are living, creative and still active within all living things, plants and animals are still adapting and evolving. God is the power behind this glorious evolution.

The Origin of Death

As we mentioned in the last chapter, many Christians think that plants and animals became predatory and defensive only after the fall of Adam and Eve. They envision a peaceful world with no death or disease before Adam and Eve sinned. They wrongly think that death is evil, and therefore, could not have been in the earth until after the sin of mankind.

To see the error in that thinking we must develop a different—more accurate—view of how God created the world as recorded in Genesis. At the end of each of the six days of creation God said that His work was good (Gen. 1:3-23). He made Adam and Eve to have dominion over the earth, and to cultivate and keep the garden.

Please note that creation needed a human being to care for it. Plants did not grow naturally in straight rows. Adam needed to cultivate the land. In other words, the natural world of vegetation was good by creation, but it could be improved upon from the perspective of being a garden.

This may seem insignificant at first, but it has profound implications. God created things which could be improved upon by man. Now, obviously, He created man, and it was in His plan to create a world which needed man. But out of the nature of God came forth created things which could grow in uncultivated ways.

This very fact contradicts some people's image of God. They perceive of a God who emanates perfection in a mechanical way. Anything which seems disorganized or imperfect they accredit to Satan or to the sin of Adam and Eve. The truth is, however, that God created nature in such a way that it could be improved. God is not a big machine which pumps out finished products. He is more like a Father who creates "unfinished things" so those He loves may have work, purpose in life, and a sense of accomplishment.

Consider an even more eye-opening fact about creation: life and death were both part of creation from the beginning.

We see this first with plant life. Hundreds of plants are "annuals," designed to live, reproduce, and then die each year. In Genesis we are told that the plants were created to be food (Gen. 1:29-30). Adam was told to eat of the seed-bearing plants and trees which bear fruit. It is impossible to consume a living seed or fruit without killing it. The human digestive tract completely breaks apart all plant cells before absorbing them. Therefore, we have to conclude that God intended from the beginning for the death of plants to be part of this world.

This is more profound when we consider animal life. Death is necessary. If just ordinary rabbits reproduced naturally with none dying, within less than 100 years every square foot of the earth would be inhabited by a living rabbit. If the beetles presently on the earth reproduced unhindered with none dying, the entire world would be covered several feet thick with beetles within 50 years. We could report similar facts about many other prolific animals. We also could point out that it is impossible for any large animal such as an elephant to walk through a forest without stepping on and crushing insects every single day.

The obvious fact is that God created animals to live and die. Death was a part of His original design.

There is a verse in the Bible which often is misused by those who want to teach just the opposite. Romans 5:12 tells us:

> *Therefore, just as through one man sin entered into the world, and death through sin, and so death spread to all men, because all sinned....*

Those who believe that there was no death in the Garden of Eden before the fall of man like to quote this verse and then emphasize that "death came through Adam."

It is true that death came through Adam; however, notice where this death spread. The death which came through Adam spread "to all men." It did not come upon the plant and animal kingdom. In fact, this verse tells us that death came upon all men because all men sin. Plants and animals do not sin. Romans 5:12 is not talking about plants and animals, but is explaining how mankind lost immortality through the sin of Adam.

Plants and animals never were created to live forever. They are of a lower nature than man, by God's design. Life and death were incorporated into their nature from the beginning.

Not only was death included by design, but animals killing and eating one another was also included. This is startling to many Christians, but a fact. Allow me to show it to you.

In the book of Job we read about a conversation that God had with Job, in which God takes credit for causing the lion to hunt and kill her prey (Job 38:39), the wild ox to be untamable (Job 39:5-12), the ostrich to treat her young cruelly (Job 39:16), the eagle to spy out food from afar while the young suck blood (Job 39:26-30), and leviathan with teeth that terrify (Job 41:14). Make no mistake about God's words: He made animals in this fashion.

Hawks spend their days hunting mice. Foxes kill rabbits. Fish eat other fish. Spiders build webs to trap and eat other bugs. Trees die of old age. Plants die. Animals die. Animals eat one another. Every day billions of animals die and billions are born. All of this is by God's design. This is how He made things. This is how things were created in the beginning.

For some time in my own life, I had difficulty dealing with this fact, because I had considered death and animals killing one another as something evil. Therefore, I reasoned that it could not have originated with God. Instead, I rationalized that these behaviors of animals were the result of sin coming into the world and/or Satan's degenerative work upon nature. Of course, creation was *"subjected to futility"* since the fall of man (Rom. 8:20), and Satan has had a degenerative influence upon the world. Diseases also have increased because of sin in the world. However, the characteristics of death and animals killing one another were created in nature from the beginning.

This contradicts some people's definition of "good." They believe God created all things good, and they reason that only good things could come forth from God. However, they never have been able to see death and animals eating one another as good. The truth is, however, that our definition of "good" needs to change.

To make this change, consider the following.

First, death from the beginning may not have entailed the pain which we associate with it today. For example, we know that God multiplied the woman's pain in childbirth after the fall. The fall of Adam and Eve released a curse upon all the world; if that curse bore the same nature as the curse upon women in childbearing, we can speculate that somehow pain was multiplied in many other areas as well. No one knows for sure, but we are considering possible consequences of the fall. Perhaps death did not entail the negative connotation nor the pain which we associate with it now.

Second, we should consider the positive fruit resulting from plant and animal death, especially before the fall of mankind.

To see this, remember what Paul wrote about different aspects of creation having different glories (I Cor. 15:41). We understand that some things are of a higher glory than others. Of course, man was created in the very image and glory of God, but we also could conclude that animals are of a greater glory than plants. If we carry this thinking through, we may say that intelligent mammals are of a higher glory than insects or other more simple creatures.

Now, consider how an animal of a lesser glory may be eaten by an animal of higher glory. In that case, to give one's life for a higher purpose is not evil. Do we even dare consider the possibility that for one form of life to be used by a higher form of life would be an honor? Yes, because in the order of creation, lower forms of life would be lifted to a higher level of glory by yielding their lives. It was God who designed the food chain.

This process of lifting things from one level of glory to another (moving up the food chain) would have been much more positive before the fall than it was after. We are told that creation was subjected to futility—implying that many things became useless—meaningless and wasteful—after the fall. Today the deaths of many animals can be considered useless, for they may die of disease or starvation in such a way that no higher forms of life benefit. However, before the curse of futility this may not have been the case. If lower forms only gave their lives for higher forms, nothing ever would have lived in futility. All would be fulfilling greater purposes for God's glory.

(A more fundamental question lies at the heart of this discussion, and that is this: "Can death bring glory?" We have implied that when an animal of lesser glory is eaten by an animal of higher glory, this is not evil, and in fact, it is good. Can we not also point out that the death of Jesus Christ brought glory to God the Father? Of course, this is true.)

Finally, we need to consider that God may have instilled the element of death and dying in nature from the beginning in order to reveal to us something about His own nature. Remember that His invisible attributes and divine nature are revealed in creation (Rom. 2:20). We like to think of God as good in the sense of being peaceful, loving, healing, helping, and never hurting anyone. But the truth is that our God is still a consuming fire (Heb. 12:29). There is an aspect of His nature which brings judgment. For us to deny completely the element of harshness in creation is to deny this aspect of His nature. We should not be afraid to embrace some element of pain, death, and finality in creation, for indeed this is also a part of who He is.

Christians who have a difficult time conceiving of a God from whom death could come need to read through the Scriptures to see the numerous incidents in which God released forces which we normally consider negative. For example, in the first book of the Bible we read that the Lord God "cursed" the earth (Gen. 5:29 and 8:21); decided to "blot out man" (Gen. 6:7), and to "destroy all flesh" (Gen. 6:17); "...struck Pharaoh and his house with great plagues...." (Gen. 12:17); made all of the women of Abimelech's house unable to bear children (Gen. 20:18); destroyed the cities of Sodom and Gomorrah (Gen. 19:24). These and similar examples are throughout the Bible.

Furthermore, God created angelic creatures able to kill and destroy. For example, the angel of the Lord went throughout Egypt killing the first-born of all those who did not mark the doorposts of their homes with the blood of a Passover lamb. Similarly the angel of the Lord destroyed the enemies of the Hebrew people on several occasions. *If the spiritual creatures which God created can induce death, we should not be surprised if the visible creatures, such as lions, foxes, hawks, sharks, and spiders, also were created with a nature to kill.*

In some ways it is difficult for us to ponder these issues, but it is inescapable if we are going to believe the Holy Scriptures. God Himself declared that He is:

> *"The One forming light and creating*
> *darkness,*
> *Causing well-being and creating*
> *calamity;*

I am the Lord who does all these."
(Is. 45:7)

Some Christians do not believe this Bible verse. They have become so set in their concept of who God is, that they cannot fit into their view this Scripture nor the numerous others which talk about destructive actions which God has taken. The truth is that God instilled death in creation from the very beginning: He created well-being and calamity.

Of course, the day will come when God's kingdom manifests fully upon this earth. Then the lion and the lamb will lie down together. Death will be done away completely. That day will come when the rulership of Jesus Christ is realized through His people taking dominion on this earth.

However, things were not created that way in the beginning. Death and dying were a part of creation. God designed a world which required man's stewardship. Of course, things have gotten worse because of the fall, but some degree of pain and death were instilled in nature from the very start. To deny this, is to deny the judgment aspect of God's nature.

Animal Life

We have referred to the glory resonating in different aspects of creation—glory which originates from the spoken Word of God. God's Words are backed by spiritual substance (discussed in Volume V, chapter six). As Jesus declared, His Words are spirit and life (John 6:63). That spirit and life was released into every aspect of creation. Therefore, when God spoke living things into existence, *spiritual substance* from God was released to permeate all the plants and animals.

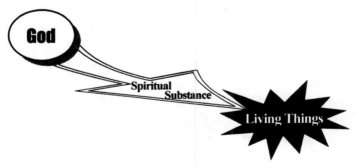

Let's look at animal life and discuss what this *spiritual substance* is that permeates their nature.

Several Old Testament passages mention the soul of an animal and tell us that its soul is in or is associated with its blood (e.g., Lev. 17:11, 14). The Hebrew word for soul in these passages is *nephesh*. Some Bible translations interpret this word *"life"* and others interpret it as *"soul."* It is important to note that the Hebrew word *nephesh* is the same word used to speak of the soul of man (e.g., Gen. 2:7). Therefore, it is correct for us to say that animals with blood have souls.

The Bible does not tell us nor imply that an animal without blood has a soul. We still can recognize a glory resident in all of God's creation; however, only the higher animals—that is, the ones with blood—are referred to as soul-bearing.

Although we recognize souls existing in higher animals, we must not think of them as equal to the soul of man. Animals were created differently than mankind. Adam was formed from the dust, and the breath of God was released into him. We are told that Adam *"became a living soul"* (Gen. 2:7 KJV). This was said in contrast to the rest of God's creation in order to distinguish Adam from animal life. The spiritual energy in Adam came from God's breath; the spiritual energy in animals came from God's spoken Word. Both higher animals and people have a soul, but the soul in an animal is different than the soul of man.

What is the function of an animal's soul?

First, the soul activates the animal's physical being, allowing it to live. When the soul leaves the body, the animal is dead. (Shortly we will explain what happens to the soul of an animal after death.)

Animals are more than mechanistic creatures acting merely out of instinct. Unfortunately, many people think of animals as creatures of habit having no emotions, thoughts of their own, or wills. Such thinking is not according to biblical revelation. Because higher animals have a soul, they have emotions, thoughts, and wills. In fact, many animals have stronger emotions than people do. For example, a dog can miss his owner when the owner is gone for an extended time period and then be overwhelmed with joy when the owner returns. Animals can love, bond, and even make decisions concerning how they act and respond to the things which happen around them. Since they have souls, they have personalities unique to themselves.

Amazingly, some animals can discern between people who have malicious intent and those who are acting justly. Dogs are especially sensitive to people who walk with authority such as the postman or policeofficer who boldly walks up to a house to do his job. Cats can sense a relaxed soul and spiritual energy peacefully flowing from it. Nature lovers have numerous stories of how various wild animals have responded to them according to their intentions. All animals respond to spiritual energy to some degree. They are a part of this creation which is both spiritual and natural in its existence.

Consider how pets respond to their owners. As an owner spends time with a pet, that animal will begin to take on characteristics of its owner. A friendly individual is more likely to produce a friendly dog. A nervous owner may produce a nervous cat. Certain animals such as dogs, cats, and horses especially are sensitive to the nature of their owners.

An amazing example of animal responsiveness is that of a man who has a feeding trough behind his house where many wild animals such as raccoons, foxes, deer, and rabbits come to eat. These natural enemies gather in peace at the trough. The man does not enforce this peace by aggressiveness, but by watching from a distance and believing that none will hurt the other. It is a fact that people's thoughts and faith influence the nature of the animals.

Animals also bond spiritually. In the wild, birds such as geese bond for life. In a home, dogs and cats often become companions. Sometimes the domestic and wild boundaries are even crossed, as when a fox becomes a playmate to a housecat.

So also, the bonds between animals and humans are real, invisible forces.

When we mention such bonds, we are not giving credence to unhealthy bonds wherein animals are raised up in importance to the level of human beings. Christians should keep in mind that animals are of a lower creation than people, and they exist for the benefit of mankind. God told mankind to *rule over* the animals (Gen. 1:28). When bonds between people and animals are allowed to rise to a place of equality there is a violation of the God-ordained order of creation. In fact, the glory of man is violated within a person who makes himself one with an animal. At the same time, we recognize that healthy bonds do form between people and animals as long as animals are kept subservient to humans. Those bonds must be held in lower priority than human-to-human relationships.

Recognizing the spiritual side of animal life, we also should discuss implications for the existence of animals in heaven, eternally, or on the new earth.

We already have mentioned that animals were not created immortal. In the previous chapter we explained how death was designed in their nature from the beginning. Even though animals have a spiritual side to their nature, they experience death, which is final: they will not live again.

However, we should not conclude that God has no purpose for animals beyond their few short days, months, or years on this earth. After God created animals, He declared them "good." God likes animals.

What, then, is the future for animal life? Recall how a curse came over the world after the fall of mankind. This curse somehow encompassed the animal kingdom and subjected it to futility and corruption. The apostle Paul explained how all of creation shall be set free from the curse when Christians come into their full inheritance in God:

> *For the anxious longing of the creation waits eagerly for the revealing of the sons of God. For the creation was subjected to futility, not of its own will, but because of Him who subjected it, in hope that the creation itself also will be set free from its slavery to corruption into the freedom of the glory of the children of God.* (Rom. 8:19-21)

Notice that God has a purpose for creation. A future is in store for plants and animals. He is not done with them.

God will make new heavens and a new earth. Christians will put on immortality and Jesus will reign from New Jerusalem. On the new earth there will be animals. They never shall have diseases nor pain. They will be subject completely to the sons of God, that is, the Christians who have entered into that eternal reward. Christians will enjoy the presence, service, and companionship of animals on the new earth.

So then, we understand that animals which have died have gone out of existence; they will not return. However, animals alive at the coming of our Lord shall go through a redemption from the curse and many will go on to live on the new earth.

Will new species of animals come into existence on the new earth? No one knows for sure, but we can rest in knowing that whatever God considers good, He will make available for the enjoyment of His children in the future.

The Even Race

Astronomers tell us that the outer limits of our universe are moving farther and farther away from us—that is, our universe is expanding. This being true, if we went back in time, our universe would be smaller. Scientists have extrapolated back and postulate that our universe would have been one united mass about twenty billion years ago. At that point many scientists say a "Big Bang" set the mass of our universe into outward motion.

Of course, this time frame easily can be challenged. Furthermore, creationists point out that we have no proof that the universe ever was one united mass. However, both Christians and non-Christians would agree that there was a specific cataclysmic starting point. Rather than calling it a Big Bang, let's call it creation—or, God spoke.

Setting aside time periods and various viewpoints, I want you to recognize the expanding direction of our universe. Both creationists and evolutionary scientists agree. Things are moving outward.

This is evidence not only of a Creator, but also of a "One who guides." Allow me to explain this *guided motion* in creation.

Think about the forward movement of living things, how plant life is reproducing, advancing, adapting, and even evolving. We accredited this positive motion to the force of God's spoken Word at creation. Atheistic biologists would prefer to accredit such forward motion to random mutation and natural selection. To see how inadequate their explanation is, envision any two plants that compete for food, water, or habitat. If random mutations were responsible for the advancement of a species, then there would be random overtaking of one species by another. Species quickly would eliminate one another and few or no species would be left.

To see this more clearly, consider viruses which live off plants. If any one of those viruses mutated to become more aggressive, it would destroy the plants upon which it lives. Atheistic biologists would say that natural selection is a self-governing force: if a virus destroyed its host then the virus too would become extinct. That explanation is inadequate because many viruses host on more than one type of plant. If any one of those billions of viruses mutated in a positive, aggressive fashion, it easily would destroy one species of host plant while allowing another to stay alive. To be successful, all it needs to do is keep one host species alive while killing all others. If random mutation was the propelling force, that is exactly what would happen: a random extinction of all living things except two—the supreme virus and its supreme host.

Here is an example from the animal kingdom. Foxes eat both mice and rabbits. If foxes randomly evolved into more efficient killers of rabbits, they would reduce the number of rabbits in the environment. Atheistic evolutionists would say that foxes never could evolve very much lest they completely destroy their food supply of rabbits. They have tried to explain that the limiting force on an animal's evolution is the fact that it would eliminate its food source, and hence, limit its own population. But that explanation is inadequate because most predatory species feed on more than one other species. There is nothing to hold back a species from evolving to the point of exterminating one species of prey and then moving on to another prey species.

This fact works throughout all the plant and animal kingdom. Things are advancing; however, there is something Bigger holding the advancement of life in check. The truth is that it is an "even race," not a random race. Advancement is being guided by something or Someone, not by random mutation.

Furthermore, we can talk about a single animal and its fight against various diseases. Bacteria and viruses are adapting, evolving, and becoming more efficient at living off host animals. At the same time each animal is adapting and becoming more efficient in fighting diseases. In this struggle they limit each other. However, if either the disease-causing entity or the host evolved much faster than the other, one would eliminate the other. This undoubtedly has happened at certain times in history, but why has this not completely eliminated all of life? Consider how much faster disease-causing bacteria should be mutating than host animals. A simple bacteria goes through thousands of reproductive cycles for every time one large animal gives birth. If the race between bacteria and host animals was determined merely by random chance, the bacteria would have billions and billions of chances to get ahead of their host. We have to conclude that there is something other than random mutation governing the race between competing species.

I dare say it is God.

We can see this "even race" also in society. We saw how all of society is moving in the direction of progress—filling the earth and subduing all things. However, no one area of progress is far in front of another. For example, at the approximate time mankind learned to communicate via telegraph, radios, and telephones, we also were learning how to travel more rapidly by means such as trains, automobiles, and then airplanes. At the time the computer technology necessary for outer space flight was being developed, the necessary discoveries in metallurgy and chemistry also were being made. Some would accredit such an even-race phenomenon to supply and demand, but there is more than that governing this progress. Imagine if mankind were two thousand years ahead in computer technology than in developing the metals necessary for satellite design. We would not be nearly as advanced as we are today.

We could talk about countless areas of society's progress. As new diseases appear, medical breakthroughs also appear. As the population of the earth booms, we learn how to produce food more efficiently. As fossil fuels become depleted, we can surmise that alternative and better sources of energy will be discovered. Things are advancing in all areas as if mankind is being guided ahead in a progressive, evenly guided direction.

All of creation is being guided. The horse is moving and Someone is holding the reins.

Life Elsewhere?

Over thirty years ago a Christian man whom I greatly respect said, "If life is ever discovered on other planets, it will be the downfall of Christianity." I agreed with him at the time, although the statement troubled me greatly. Today, I am no longer troubled. Allow me to explain.

People once thought that the sun and stars revolved around the earth. This worldview fit their perception as they looked with the unaided eye into the skies. It also seemed to match the traditional Christian worldview which saw mankind as the center of the universe. That worldview, however, became shaken when men like Galileo declared that the earth and other planets revolved around the sun. It was not only scientists who had to wrestle with this discovery, but theologians had to scramble to readjust their Christian worldview.

Similarly, when Columbus and others discovered unknown regions of the world, Christian leaders had to expand their view of God. Before such discoveries, it was easier for people to think of God looking down and exclusively watching over their lives. When new people groups were discovered, Christians had to step back and envision a bigger God who always had His eyes not just on them, but on all people with a purpose and destiny for their lives.

When such discoveries have been made, some Christian leaders have resisted the facts as presented by scientists, pioneers, or others on the forefront of discovery. However, in time, Christians expanded their view of God and their perspective of the Holy Scriptures.

It is time we ask what would happen to our present worldview if life on other planets were discovered. We are not saying that life does exist on other planets. We are just looking at our own worldview and seeing if it could embrace such a discovery if it were presented to us in the future.

It starts with our concept of God. In this book we have emphasized the creative, life-giving nature of God. We have seen how His spoken Words not only create, but go on producing life. All of creation declares who He is. Among other attributes, we have found Him to be the Source emanating life, detail, abundance, and immensity.

What does this mean? Compare it with works done by humans on this earth. Bill Gates, for example, is leading many computer advancements. If we were to hear of some new item he produced, we would expect it to be ingenious and fill some niche in the technological world. We would think this because we know what type of things Bill Gates produces.

In the same way, all the universe is declaring the nature of God. Since He created the solar systems, galaxies, black holes, and universes yet undiscovered, we should expect them to bear His nature. God is not dead, but alive—full of life; the very Source of Life. Rather than ask, "Can there be life on other planets," from our knowledge of God we should ask, "Is it conceivable for God to have created the universe without life bursting from His nature?" Of course, He could have created it sterile by choice, but that is not what we learn of His nature from the Scriptures, nor from the world we already have discovered. It is much more reasonable to believe that life permeates the universe.

Yes, I dare say that it is conceivable for life to be on other planets. I am not saying human life, but truly living creatures. From what we know about God, that is the kind of thing that flows out of His nature.

Does our understanding from the Bible allow this? Genesis starts off saying:

> *In the beginning God created the heavens and the earth. And the earth was formless and void....*
> (Gen. 1:1-2)

Notice that the *earth* was formless and void. It does not say that the rest of the universe was formless and void. Furthermore, this introduction to the Bible implies that the Book we have been given is a description of God's workings on our planet earth. Yes, God changed it from void to life. But we are told nothing of what God did on other planets. To positively say He did or did not create living things elsewhere is to add to Scripture.

Next, we need to analyze our view of God's relationship to mankind. The traditional Christian worldview has seen God's attention as centered on us. As we mentioned earlier, each time new people groups were discovered in history, Christians had to step back and envision a bigger God who had His eyes not just on them, but on all people with a purpose and destiny for their lives. If, indeed, life were discovered on other planets, we would have to step further back and see a God who encompasses all creatures. In fact, I dare say that we would have to see the center of the universe not as God's relationship to man, but as God Himself. *He* would be the center, rather than the view which sees man as the center or God's relationship to man as the center.

Now, in saying all this, we are not lessening the significance of God's unique relationship to man. Man was created in God's image—distinct and different than plant or animal life. Man is further elevated when we contemplate God's love in sending His own Son to die for us. Indeed, people who respond to the Gospel will dwell with Him forever.

Without lessening that unique and highest place for man, can we conceive of life elsewhere? When biologists discover some new animal on a remote part of this earth, does it lessen our relationship with God? Indeed, it glorifies Him, magnifying His abundance and greatness. Similarly, if life were discovered on other planets, we should be more awed by His greatness.

This is further amplified when we see God-the-Father's relationship to the Son as more central to the universe than God's relationship to man. In other words, is this universe created for man or for Jesus? Colossians 1:16 tells us:

> *For by Him* [Jesus] *all things were created, both in the heavens and on earth, visible and invisible, whether thrones or dominions or rulers or authorities—all things have been created by Him and for Him.*

Jesus was the co-creator with the Father. They did it together—as One. However, the Father's heart was to bless the Son. It was all created for Jesus.

This truth is important because as long as we wrongly think that creation exists for man, we will limit our thinking and see no purpose in God creating anything in other solar systems which mankind never may discover and enjoy. However, since this universe was created for the Son, it is irrelevant whether or not man ever discovers the depth or extent of the universe. More importantly, since the universe is God's gift to the Son, we have to believe that it is extravagant—wonderful beyond our wildest dreams. That is how the Father loves the Son.

A major reason some Christians never could conceive of life elsewhere is because they have an unbiblical view of the universe. They wrongly think it was created for man. When we correct our thinking in this area, it makes room for God's creation beyond man's limitations. Again I say, the universe was created for the Son. How much could He embrace and enjoy? Picture how a human being can walk through a garden and enjoy the pleasures it offers. Now picture our Lord Jesus. Is He limited to walk on this earth and enjoy only the gardens here? The universe is about His pleasure, not ours.

Someday man may discover life on other planets. If life is there, it is conceivable that God would allow His children, whom He also loves, to experience it with the Son. However, the primary purpose of the universe is for *His* pleasure.

Even though we are developing a bigger, more biblical view of the universe, we still need to keep in mind the central position man holds in God's heart. He does love us. The Son died not for the animals on this planet nor for the living things—if they exist—on other planets. He died for us. We hold a central place in God's heart, but the universe does not exist exclusively for us.

Only with that biblical perspective can we answer the question, "Could there be life elsewhere?"

Now, would it be possible for non-carbon-based life to exist? To understand this question, let me explain that life on our planet is carbon-based because the element carbon is the basic building block of all living things. Furthermore, the chemical reaction of carbon combined with oxygen is at the base of all energy used by plants and animals here.

Scientists have not yet been able to conceive of a way in which non-carbon-based life could exist. We do not know any other way in which large amounts of energy readily could be available for plants, animals, or other living creatures. For this reason, when scientists investigate the possibility of life existing elsewhere, they tend to look at planets which have similar environmental conditions to earth. They look for planets with water and temperatures similar to ours, along with an abundance of carbon in the atmosphere. This is reasonable from the scientific point of view because of our present understanding of life.

However, from the biblical point of view should we limit our thinking only to carbon-based life? God is spirit. Out of His creative nature can flow unlimited forms of life. From a theological point of view it would be just as conceivable for God to create life on Venus in an atmosphere filled with sulfuric acid, or Jupiter with an atmosphere reaching thousands of degrees Celsius. Furthermore, God does not need a planet on which to base living creatures. They could flow from His nature into space itself. Indeed, if we discovered such life, we would have to conclude that God's ways are much higher than our ways, and that He is bigger than we previously thought. What a concept!

The idea of finding life elsewhere troubles many Christians because they wrongly think such a discovery would prove the theory of evolution. Just the opposite is the case. Scientists know that the probabilities of life evolving only by the processes of chance mutation and natural selection are infinitely small. The probabilities of it happening twice are even smaller. The more life that exists out there, the less likely that evolution could be the source. (Now I am not implying that evolution ever could account for even a single living thing, because, as I have explained, God created plants and animals on this planet in distinct kinds.) Because of the mathematical improbabilities, the more life we discover on other planets, the more assuredly we will know that the theory of evolution is wrong.

In conclusion, we ask once again, is there life elsewhere? To date it neither has been proven nor disproven. However, if life is discovered, it will not surprise me. In fact, as a Christian who sees a life-giving God as the center of all things and the relationship of the Father to the Son as the primary purpose for the universe, I expect life to be elsewhere—not human life—but, indeed, living, beautiful, awesome creatures.

Spirit Beings

Our discussion of living things is not complete unless we talk about the existence of invisible and/or spiritual creatures. We do not know when these were created for they are not mentioned in the book of Genesis during the first six days. However, the Bible does teach us certain things about spiritual beings.

Read Colossians 1:16 again:

> *For by Him all things were created, both in the heavens and on earth, visible and invisible, whether thrones or dominions or rulers or authorities—all things have been created by Him and for Him.*

What things—visible and invisible—did He create in the heavens? They have some association with thrones, dominions, rulers, or authorities. This implies that there are living entities in the heavens—and not just a few, but many.

We are talking about more than the existence of angels. Traditional Christianity has held to a belief in angels—that is, they believe in friendly creatures with wings that float around in white gowns and sometimes even reveal themselves in human form. We also are speaking of more than demons or the devil. Of course, we believe these exist. However, there are other spiritual creatures out there.

For example, Ezekiel 1 describes four living creatures each having four faces and four wings. Their legs are straight and their feet are like bronze calf's hooves. Under their wings are human-like hands. Their faces are like that of a man, a lion, a bull, and an eagle. Each of these four creatures moves in unison in the middle of wheels where fire flashes to and fro. The wheels extend from earth to the throne of God. So awesome is the sight that it produces terror.

These creatures are real. We are not alone.

We have no way of knowing how many other living creatures have been created by God; however, it is wrong to limit our understanding to angels, demons, man, and animals. The book of Revelation shows us other images of creatures which exist (e.g., Rev. 4 and 9). To limit our understanding of angels to pretty white creatures with wings is contrary to what we are shown in the Bible. There is more. Yes, there are more categories of creatures out there.

Jude 1:6 tells us:

And angels who did not keep their

own domain, but abandoned their
proper abode, He has kept in eternal
bonds under darkness for the judg-
ment of the great day.

To understand biblical references to angels, note that the word *angel* (*aggelos* in Greek) is used for spiritual creatures that are both good and bad. In our modern terminology we usually call bad angels demons or devils, but in the Bible the word *angel* is used for either.

Notice that the angels (demons) to which I referred in the last quoted passage left their proper abode. This implies that angels have a will. They decide to obey or disobey God.

Many Christians wrongly have thought of angels as spiritual robots, acting very machine-like in their obedience to God. That is not Scriptural. Of course, the devil disobeys God, but all the angels, good and bad, have a free will.

Furthermore, they experience emotions. For example, the good angels rejoice when a person repents (Luke 15:10). Angels have desires—some of them unmet. For example, God's angels long to understand the joy of salvation which people can experience (I Peter 1:12).

This concept of angels as *free agents* with their own thoughts and desires is important in our understanding of God's creatures. I Corinthians 6:3 reminds us, *"Do you not know that we shall judge angels?"* The future judgment of angels implies that they can choose to serve God or not. Angels are not spiritual robots. Rather they are real creatures with emotions and desires, able to make decisions on their own.

Angels (good or bad) seem to have assigned locations or specific tasks on this earth. Jude 1:6 says some angels left their proper abode. This implies that they were assigned specific locations. It seems a significant point in God's order that these creatures maintain their assigned dwelling places.

Some angels are assigned to watch over individual people (Matt. 4:6; 18:10). Other angels carry out specific tasks or assignments given to them by God (Ps. 103:20). Hebrews 1:14 tells us about angels which come to dwell on this earth and are *"sent out to render service for the sake of those who will inherit salvation."* Other angels move back and forth, descending to the earth and then ascending back to heaven (Gen. 28:12; John 1:51).

Although angels work on earth, the earth exists for man. We were put in charge here (Gen. 1:28). When Adam yielded to Satan, Satan became the prince of the power of the air. Now, as man yields to Satan, Satan can act and influence this realm. Demons may try to deceive people and get them to follow their evil desires. However, it is still true that man has God-given authority upon this earth.

When we talk about creatures from other dwelling places, it is important to keep in mind that we have authority here. They cannot come and do whatever they want to do on this earth (unless, of course, God has commissioned them to intervene in the affairs of mankind). As we understand from Jude 1:6, some creatures have violated the God-ordained order and left their assigned dwelling places. However, this is in violation of the fact that the earth was given for mankind to rule.

This gives us an important point when we consider the existence of aliens and UFO sightings. Should Christians believe in their existence? Are such things real? If so, how should we react?

We should not be so naive as to believe all of the sightings of UFO's reported in tabloid magazines or mystery-type television programs. Personally, I am skeptical of spacecraft-type reportings. I think the vast majority of such sightings are imagined or fraudulent. If there are truly intelligent beings riding in flying objects and visiting our world, it remains to be proven.

I am more open to think there are (on rare occasions) spiritual creatures momentarily manifesting in our atmosphere. Some may be demons showing themselves in order to deceive people. Some may be spirit-beings leaving their assigned dwelling places. Others may be good angels manifesting for some reason or other. Or there may even be appearances of other created beings which we cannot even label yet.

Whatever they are, our attitude toward such beings should be one of dominion and authority. This is our planet. They have no authority here.

Unfortunately, many people do not understand God-delegated authority. They even may be yielding human authority to such creatures unknowingly. For example, when people spend time pondering the existence of such beings, there can arise in their minds and hearts anticipation and fear that such beings will appear. Anticipation is a form of faith. Fear is faith that negative things will happen. Any such faith may give room for visible or invisible entities to enter our realm. That is the authority we have as human beings. For this reason, people who are most fearful or most expectant are most likely to encounter such phenomena.

Again, let me say that the vast majority of UFO sightings are imagined or fraudulent. However, there are some that, indeed, may be valid appearances of creatures not meant to dwell in our world.

Before we leave this subject, it is worth mentioning that God's created order is established with all living things. In chapter seven we mentioned how it is a violation of God's order for people to bond on an equal level with animals. Similarly, creatures or beings that exist elsewhere are of a different glory than man, and for man to develop relationships of an equal level with them also violates ordained order.

Even when people focus too much attention on angels, there is a violation of God's plans and purposes. I have dealt with several situations where Christian individuals or groups became oriented toward angelic manifestations. In each case, some form of destructive element entered into the situation in a short time and people were hurt. The dynamics became non-glorifying to God in one way or another. This is not to say that reported angelic manifestations are unreal. Indeed, some of them are real. However, even in the Bible encounters between angels and men were always short-lived. In my experience to date, I have not seen any long-term or repeated manifestations of angels which produced positive fruit.

I have come to believe that this is the result of God-ordained order. We have a jealous God who will not allow our attentions and affections to be fixed on creatures of other glories. Angels are created as agents to serve God and carry out His commands (Ps. 103:20). When we violate God's purposes, we violate a sacred order which He has established.

This is also true for life forms existing outside of this planet. Indeed, my worldview developed from the Bible and an understanding of who God is, does have room for the existence of extraterrestrials, visible and invisible. However, I do not believe that man's focus should be upon them. Nor should we allow them access to our realm by our meditations and faith. They have a purpose in God which we may discover in the future; however, we must not violate God's purposes for their and our existence.

11

Matter, Space, Light, and Laws

Colossians 1:16 tells us that Jesus was the co-Creator of all things with the Father. The verse which immediately follows gives us an additional truth concerning Jesus' role in creation:

And He is before all things, and in Him all things hold together.
(Col. 1:17)

Note our Lord Jesus' ongoing role: He is presently holding all things together.

This is fascinating because one of the unsolved mysteries of the universe is: "What holds things together?" Scientists have been intrigued by the nature of gravity and the other forces of attraction.

What holds the moon in its orbit around the earth? We can answer: "the force of gravity between the earth and the moon," but that is really no answer at all, because *gravity* is just a word used to label a force which no one can explain. The originators of this word just as easily could have used any other combination of letters, such as *abcd* or *xyz*. By labeling something, we have not explained it. As yet, science can offer no explanation for why the moon does not fly off into outer space, why the planets remain in orbit around the sun, or why you are held onto the surface of this earth.

The unexplained forces of attraction go deeper into every molecule and atom in our universe. What holds atoms together? What holds electrons in their orbit around a nucleus? What holds the nucleus together? What is magnetism? If we answer these questions by saying "the power of attraction," we really have not answered the questions, but only *labeled* something which we do not understand. Even if we say "atomic attraction," "nuclear attraction," or "positive and negative charges," we have not given answers because these, too, are merely labels masking the deeper question: "What is it?"

The Bible tells us: *in Him all things hold together*.

Indeed, these forces are great. The thought of holding the moon in its orbit is awesome. The idea of sustaining stars in their locations is beyond human comprehension. Even discoveries in atomic and nuclear energy reveal that the bonds holding subatomic particles together are so great that if a few are broken tremendous power is released.

Where did this power originate? Scientists can label it, study it, and measure it, but no one can explain from whence it comes—apart from

God. That is one of the most amazing features of the Bible. It speaks where science stops.

Consider matter and space. Of course, material things can be broken down into molecules, and molecules into atoms. Even atoms can be studied and scientists know many things about particles within atoms. However, there is a deeper question. From where did the *stuff of creation* come in the first place? Why is there anything? We can postulate about an expanding universe and theorize about black holes in outer space, but who can explain the existence of matter and space?

These are the first questions which the Bible answers:

> *In the beginning God created the heavens and the earth.* (Gen. 1:1)

There are philosophers who have postulated alternative possibilities for the existence of matter and space, but they immediately leave science, because science is, by definition, the discovery of truth by observing evidence. There never has been evidence beyond the point of God's contact with this world. We can study matter and space, but we do not know where they originated, apart from God.

The same can be said about light. What is light? We know it acts like a wave in some ways, and like a particle in other ways. We can describe how it acts, but we cannot say what light is. Nor can we say what is the origin of light.

Genesis 1:3 tells us:

Then God said, "Let there be light";
and there was light.

Light came from the spoken Word of God.

Each of these elements of our universe—gravity, matter, space, and light—find their source in Him. For this reason, we can say that these are basic elements of our universe.

For this reason, man never has been able to break gravity into smaller components and describe its constituent parts. Similarly, atoms can be broken apart and the smaller particles labeled; however, we still have the basic substance of matter. Space and light are basic building blocks of our universe, finding their source in God. He and His spoken Word are always at the heart of our deepest, most profound discoveries.

Just as significant are the *laws* which govern the physical universe. We have mentioned the law of gravity, but let's add the other Newtonian laws. We use this terminology, *Newtonian laws*, because Isaac Newton was one of the foremost scientists defining physical laws, such as the law of gravity. We would include in Newtonian laws the law of inertia which, simply stated, means that an object in motion tends to continue in motion. Also, the law that for every action there is an equal and opposite reaction; in practical, layman terms, this simply means push something and it will move. Also, the law of increasing entropy, which we discussed earlier. We know that these Newtonian laws are real. We can see them governing our universe.

The deeper and more profound question is, "Why does everything follow such laws?" Scientists can observe the order of the universe. They cannot deny that things follow such laws, but scientists cannot say from whence these laws came. Who enacted them? What is their Source? Why are there laws?

Logic tells us that there can be no design without a Designer. Every aspect of creation reveals more of the Creator, and the order of the universe tells us of an orderly God. He is there. Creation declares it.

The Nature of Time

Perhaps the most interesting laws have to do with those involving *time*. Just as the law of gravity holds us to the earth, so also in time we are confined to the present. We live in this confinement. We are unable to escape it.

Who enclosed us in this cage? Why does time exist? Who made the law?

The first words of our Bible say:

> *In the beginning God created....*
> (Gen. 1:1)

This implies that there was *a beginning*. Furthermore, it reveals to us a God who exists on the other side of the beginning. He reached into this realm and created our world within the confines of this thing we call *time*.

Some cultures in the world do not have the same concept of time that we do in the modern Western world. For example, many ancient peoples thought of time as cyclic rather than linear. Because they watched the world around them repeating itself seasonally or annually, with one generation following another, they tended to think of time as repeating itself over and over again. It was not until cultures began building and accumulating things long-term that they began to think of time advancing in a more straight-line fashion.

The cyclic way of thinking is difficult for most of us to relate to today since we have been so programmed to our linear view of life. However, take a moment to think along these lines because there are certain truths which only can be understood through the cyclic frame of mind.

Consider the Hebrew people in Bible days. They saw time in both a cyclic and a linear fashion. The cyclic element can be seen in their view of certain events repeated every week, every month, and every year. For example, when God blessed the seventh day, He did it one time, but His blessing reached through all the weeks to follow and actually released a blessing onto every future Sabbath day. In the Hebrew mind, God's blessing compared with a person yelling into the mountains and hearing the echo repeatedly as sound waves bounce off one set of mountains and then another. In similar fashion, they think of God's spoken blessing as resounding repeatedly every Sabbath throughout all of time.

With the same frame of mind, the Hebrews celebrated certain feasts on established days of the year. However, they did not see themselves as celebrating the feast independently of the generations before them. Because they celebrated on the same days of the year, they saw themselves united with those who had done so in preceding years.

In our modern Western mind-set we do not have such deep attachments to cyclic time. We see this year's celebrations as separate from last year's. We think linearly.

Our way of thinking serves us well; however, there are certain truths that we miss. There are indeed cyclic events which resonate throughout linear time. For example, when a person loses a loved one, he may re-experience related emotions at the same time every year for decades. In our Western linear way of thinking, we would accredit such experiences to the other events of the person's life which they psychologically associate with the death of their loved one. However, I dare say that there is more to it than that. Time, indeed, does have a cyclic nature to some degree, and there does exist a recurring echo of significant events.

This includes not just negative experiences, but also positive ones. An individual may accomplish some great feat on a certain day of the year. It is common that other accomplishments will be made by that person or others to follow at the same time of year in the years to follow. It is as if an energy, a power, or a grace is present on that day of the year for further advancements.

The cyclic way of thinking sees time moving forward like sound waves in a rhythmic pattern. The same things are repeated weekly, monthly, or annually. It is true that some things do resonate in specific periods of time.

This makes sense when we realize that creation reveals the nature of God. Other things that He created, such as music, light, electricity, seasons, vibrations, the movement of our solar system...(perhaps everything He created) all have a rhythmic nature to them. Seeing this, we should not be surprised that time also has an inherent cyclic pattern.

Yes, time is both cyclic and linear.

Enough said about the flow of time. Let's go on to discuss another area of time important for our understanding of the whole of creation. We have taught about the theory of evolution versus the teachings of creationists. Here is another area where we see great discrepancies in what people believe.

To determine the time of creation, creationists add up the family lineages as recorded in the Bible and set Adam's beginning at 6,000 years ago. Evolutionists typically assign the beginning of this earth at 5 billion years ago and the beginning of the universe at 20 billion years ago when a "big bang" started it all. The difference in these views is vast. For comparison's sake, let's say that the creationists' 6,000 years were represented by a line one foot long. Five billion years then would be a line extending 158 miles. Obviously, the creationist and the evolutionist have some huge discrepancies in their views.

I already have told you that I believe the Bible but I have parted from some of the traditional creationists' views. I do believe that Adam was on this earth only a few thousand years ago.

However, I have had to wrestle with some major issues on this subject of time. The biggest has to do with Einstein's discoveries encapsulated in the formula, $E=MC^2$. Einstein taught us that *time is relative*. Einstein showed that as one approaches the speed of light, time slows down. This concept is basic to those who have studied in this field, yet profound to the rest of us who never have been exposed to it.

To understand this, consider how light travels. The light bouncing around the room where you are sitting right now is traveling so fast that you cannot even tell that it is moving. Everything seems to be lit up instantaneously. However, when we talk about very large distances, we can measure more easily how light actually does travel from place to place. For example, the light from the sun takes approximately eight minutes to reach earth.

Keeping in mind that light moves through space, consider the light which is bouncing off a clock and reaching your eyes so you can see the time on the clock. Imagine the clock tells you that it is now 3:00 PM. The light bouncing off the clock and coming toward your eyes is moving so fast that it seems to be instantaneous. But what if you were to move away from the clock at the same speed that the light is coming toward your eyes? For example, think of yourself now in a spacecraft flying away from the earth at the same speed which light travels. If you could look back to the earth and watch the same clock, it would read 3:00 PM. Because you are moving at the same speed which the light is moving, the clock would always say 3:00 PM. It would appear that time is standing still.

Now if you were to speed up faster than the speed of light and if your eyes were still able to watch the clock, that clock would appear to move backward.

This illustration is not a scientific experiment and it does not *prove* anything about time; however, it helps people form thoughts about the possibility of moving into the past, if indeed we could move faster than the speed of light. Einstein's work was much deeper than what this simple discussion proposes. We simply are helping you formulate thoughts about the possibility of time being relative.

Apply this to our understanding of creation. Picture God speaking things into existence. If His Words proceeded from His mouth and the created world manifested moving faster than the speed of light (which is very reasonable for us to think), then creation itself would extend into the past. The point when things came to rest in time actually would be before they were spoken into existence. The greater the force behind God's Words, the farther into the past creation would be thrown. If, indeed, God spoke 6,000 years ago and creation exploded in power from His Spirit, the world could have transcended time and "materialized" in the distant past—even 5 billion years ago.

Yes, Genesis chapter one could have taken place 6,000 years ago, and all things could have come into being billions of years before that date. With our present understanding of time being relative, this is possible.

What Possibly Happened?

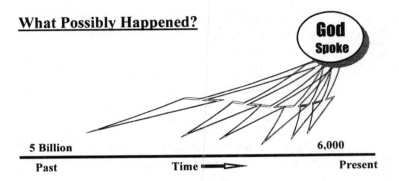

5 Billion		6,000
Past	Time ▬▷	Present

There are other explanations which Bible students and scholars have offered to explain the huge time discrepancies between the literal account of the Bible and that which is taught by evolutionists.* The explanation I offer is not presented as the final word concerning what really happened. I wasn't there. I don't know. Other teachers have reasonable explanations of what could have occurred. The explanation I have just presented is simply one very real possibility.

Some of my traditional creationist friends may abandon me at this point because they so strongly believe that the whole universe with all of life on planet earth came into existence only a few thousand years ago. They would see any

---

* Other views, including the Gap Theory and the Day-Age Theory, are held by many Christians today; however, I believe the view presented here is more logical and consistent with Scripture and present scientific evidence.

allowance for the possibility of an old earth as denying the faith. Allow me to reassure them that I believe the Bible fully.

I always have been one who considers the Bible as more accurate, reliable, and trustworthy than present scientific understanding. If I have to choose between believing the earth is 6,000 years old or believing the earth is 5 billion years old, I will choose the first. However, with our present understanding of time, I don't have to choose. Genesis one could have happened 6,000 years ago, and the earth could be 5 billion years old. Both may be true simultaneously.

Not only is this within our present understanding of time, it is also within our understanding of the Almighty Creator who acts outside of time. Even if He did not speak things into existence faster than the speed of light, He may have simply transcended time. He even can do something today and place that action in the distant past. He is God! He can act outside the limits of time and position things wherever and whenever He chooses. It is not difficult for Him. To think that the actions of God 6,000 years ago, are limited to results 6,000 years ago is to put limits on God which deny His eternal nature and divine attributes. That would be foolish and wrong.

Quantum Mechanics

Our discussion of creation is not complete without touching the topic of quantum mechanics. Perhaps we should have started here since the implications are so profound. I am not writing as someone who is actually qualified on this topic, but only as a distant, interested observer.

In the field of quantum mechanics, scientists have attempted to divide matter into its tiniest parts and then observe how they work. Many studies have been done on electrons; however, quantum physicists have also looked at smaller particles to see how they move and interact. Those who study in this field use the name "quark" to identify one of the tiniest particles.* Quantum physicists are investigating how quarks work, what governs them—what are the mechanics of a quark—and therefore, what governs the universe at its basic substance.

This is where the most amazing, baffling discoveries in science have been made in our

---

* Investigations are being done on other small particles, but they are beyond the scope of our discussion.

times. We can compare the implications of these discoveries to the discovery of the New World in the fifteenth century. So revolutionary are these findings that they are changing everything we understand about the world around us.

Many experiments and discoveries are being made in the area of quantum mechanics, but let's mention three significant to our discussion.

First is the discovery that when a quantum physicist tries to locate a single quark, it tends to appear *where he thinks it will appear*. To see this, picture a single quark moving through space. Quarks are constantly changing from waves into particles and then back into waves. When the scientist focuses on a single quark, it tends to "materialize" and become a particle in that location. As amazing as this sounds, it is true. These experiments can be repeated over and over again with the same results. Matter at its tiniest level tends to respond to the thoughts of humans.

When we consider how quarks respond to the thoughts of people, we can see how profoundly this matches the biblical understanding of the created world. Many Bible verses could be brought to our attention at this point but just consider how faith is the *substance* of things hoped for (Heb. 11:1 KJV). Our Lord explained that if we have faith as a mustard seed—which is the smallest of all seeds—we can command a mountain to move and it will obey (Matt. 17:20). Amazingly, quantum physicists have discovered that the tiniest of all particles do, indeed, respond to our thoughts.

In light of this discovery and others, quantum physicists sometimes think in terms of the whole universe acting like a thought. Indeed, we know that the whole world originated from God's thoughts and was created by His spoken Word (Heb. 11:3).

A second, and just as profound, discovery of modern quantum mechanics is this. When two particles which have been in close association with one another are separated, they continue to influence each other. For example, think of two electrons orbiting the same nucleus. Separate those two electrons from one another and alter the orientation or movement of one electron. The other electron also will be altered in its orientation and/or movement, even if it is far removed from the first. There continues to be some type of bond or influence between previously associated particles which later are separated.

This "law of influence" involves more than just one or two particles. Many scientists now believe that the entire universe is connected. Every particle influences other particles. You cannot change one particle without re-orienting a "world of associated particles."

A third discovery of quantum physicists is that *space is not empty*. To see this, consider what we just discussed about previously associated particles influencing each other. Since others move when one moves, there must be some bond, some invisible form of communication, some force being exerted between particles. This force reaches across space. What we have to conclude is that the space, which we once thought was empty, is not empty. There is something filling space.

These discoveries have led to a major shift in the scientists' understanding of the universe. Years ago when most of us first learned about atoms, we were taught that electrons orbited around nuclei with empty space filling the voids. Today quantum physicists no longer believe that what we used to think of as empty space is really empty. There is something filling all space. In fact, the focus of some studies today is not on the particles of matter, but on the space between the particles.

In the past, scientists thought that the universe followed Newtonian laws. With recent discoveries in quantum mechanics we realize that these Newtonian laws do not apply on the subatomic level.* Rather, the smallest particles are influenced by the thoughts of man and their associations with other particles. At the subatomic level things are governed by quantum laws—the ones we have mentioned and others which have not been discovered even yet.

Some people with spiritual interests have investigated these scientific truths and wrongly concluded that the quantum world is the spiritual world. That is not correct because waves and

---

* In addition, Newtonian laws do not seem to apply when speaking of things so big that they are beyond our normal grasp. For example, studies in astronomy reveal that black holes and other mega-anomalies are not governed by Newtonian laws. The law of gravity changes and time may even be distorted in ways which we have not yet comprehended.

particles are still elements of this natural world. It is better to think of the realm of angels, demons, and God as even deeper, that is, on the other side of the quantum world.

Studies in quantum mechanics indicate that the spiritual world and the natural world are *integrated*. What happens in one world influences what happens in the other. The thoughts of people actually do alter the universe. Now we have evidence that the very substance of the universe is influenced by spiritual dynamics.

An Integrated World

Seeing the natural world and the spiritual world as *integrated* puts many Bible concepts into a new light.

For example, we more easily can see how physical things can possess spiritual and moral value. The Bible refers to things and places being desecrated—being made unholy—by thoughts and activities of mankind. In contrast, God tells His people that if they repent, pray, and seek His face, He *"will heal their land"* (II Chron. 7:14). The idea that land can hold spiritual value can be understood as we see the direct influence men's thoughts, relationships, and actions have upon the universe around them.

We also can see how the thoughts of people influence and even change physical things. Of course, faith moves mountains, but let's start on a smaller, yet more significant and far-reaching scale: how faith and thoughts alter reproduction and the generations to follow.

For example, consider a married couple unable to have children. After many years of trying, they may decide to adopt a child. What has been seen in cases too numerous to be mere chance is that the couple will conceive a child soon after they adopt one. Before adopting the child, their own thought patterns—perhaps stresses associated with not being able to conceive—were in some way hindering them from conceiving a child.

A more profound example of thoughts influencing reproduction can be seen in the Bible. Consider how Jacob influenced the breeding and offspring of lambs as recorded in Genesis 30:37-43. Jacob wanted the flock to produce white spotted, striped and speckled lambs, rather than solid black ones. In order to cause this, he took sticks from trees, peeled them, and inserted them in the soil around the flocks so the sheep would see them. This caused the sheep to breed and produce more speckled, striped, and spotted lambs.

This account is baffling to evolutionary biologists because they believe that genetic variety results from chance alone. According to present biological studies, staring at white-striped sticks will not produce white-striped sheep.

If we believe the Bible, we have to conclude that Jacob knew something which present-day evolutionary biologists do not. Picture Jacob positioning white sticks all around the sheep. Somehow the sight of those sticks caused the sheep to reproduce more spotted and speckled lambs. It could have been the sheep staring at the sticks, or it could have been Jacob staring at them, or perhaps it was Jacob's belief that his actions would produce more spotted and speckled lambs. Whatever the cause, it worked.

This is biblical evidence of how the visions, thoughts, and/or beliefs of living things influence reproduction and variety within offspring. Now fit this into recent discoveries in quantum mechanics. Our thoughts influence matter at the smallest level. The biblical account of Jacob and the sheep implies that visions and thoughts can influence even reproduction and/or the genetic code within living things.

This brings us to a form of "Lamarckian Evolution." We use this terminology because a scientist name Chevalier de Lamarck (1744-1829) taught that animals may change genetically according to their desires and struggles to survive. Lamarck, for example, taught that a giraffe's neck grew longer and longer as it attempted to reach higher into the trees to find food. Charles Darwin (and evolutionary biologists today) rejected Lamarck's view in favor of the idea that change was only the result of chance mutation and natural selection. They would explain that the giraffe's desire or straining to reach higher had nothing to do with changing its genetic code, but rather chance mutation produced many varieties of giraffes, some with longer necks and some with shorter necks. The longer-necked ones simply survived because they had a survival advantage over the shorter-necked giraffes. The difference is that Lamarck taught that the giraffe's desires, rather than chance mutation alone, changed its genetic code.

In giving some credence to Lamarckian evolution we are not saying that an animal's desires are the sole source of change. As taught in chapter four, there is a force of life released by God into creation. This is the most powerful force acting upon living things to move them in a positive direction. Here we simply are adding to this truth an understanding of the influence a living organism can have on its own genetic code.

Evolutionary biologists have been teaching for over a century that living organisms cannot change their genetic code by their desires, visions, or behavior. Now with studies in quantum mechanics, scientists have concluded that man's thoughts do, indeed, alter matter at the subatomic level. We are applying this discovery of quantum physics to our understanding of biology and considering the possibility that living things may, indeed, influence their own genetic code. The biblical account of Jacob and the sheep implies this, telling us that thoughts, behavior, visions, and/or beliefs do influence offspring.

For further evidence of this, consider God's dealings with sinful mankind in the Old Testament. In some cases, He demanded that individuals *and their offspring* be put to death for the purpose of cleansing the nation (e.g., Num. 16:27-32). This seems extreme if sin is only outer behavior or simply a matter of one's personal decisions. Certain sins reach deeper within a person. For example, Romans 1:27 tells us that people who give themselves over to homosexual behavior receive *"...in their own persons the due penalty of their error."* Indeed, present research indicates that some sin tendencies are inherited genetically. Only if we accept the idea that sin can influence our very makeup does it make sense that God would at times demand that sinful people be cut off along with the generations after them.

(In pointing this out, we are not implying that it is right to cleanse society by killing groups of people. We understand that through Jesus Christ it is possible to be adopted into a new family—the family of God. If we accept that sin can influence the genetic makeup, then we also should accept that repentance can, as well.)

The main point is that visions, thoughts, desires, beliefs, and moral behavior can influence the physical world. This goes beyond living things. Scientific evidence indicates that everything around us is influenced, as well. Biblical evidence agrees. I Timothy 4:4 tells us that *everything* is sanctified by the Word of God and prayer. Physical things do carry spiritual value, and we do influence them positively or negatively.

Now develop a bigger picture. Think about the whole earth. Remember God said, *"Let the earth bring forth living creatures...."* Since spiritual value can be deposited within matter, the earth itself must bear the energy of God to produce living things.

This gives some biblical credence to the idea of "Mother Earth." Now, obviously, we do not want to go to the foolish extreme of worshipping "Mother Nature." The earth has no will nor personality of its own. However, as Christians, we should acknowledge the fact that God has released an energy into the earth. When God said, *"Let the earth bring forth....,"* His Words were directed toward the earth. His Words released energy and created a response in the earth itself. Therefore, it is biblically accurate to think of God's glory resonating from the earth.

As a womb is able to receive a seed and nurture life, so also the earth has a quality of receptivity and nurturing. Glory can be felt in a handful of soil, rich in minerals. To lie on the ground and smell its freshness can revitalize a person. To work in a garden can spiritually invigorate an exhausted soul. The earth itself is resonating with the spirit and life of God's Words.

Not just the earth but the whole of creation resonates with God's nature. It responds to the thoughts, beliefs, visions, and behavior of people.

Jesus Christ taught that the thoughts and words of people are like seeds being planted in the soil. In Mark 4:28 He explained how those seeds grow:

> *"The soil produces the crops by itself;*
> *first the blade, then the head, then*
> *the mature grain in the head."*

In another parable our Lord explained how both good and bad seeds are sown in the soil and eventually grow up to yield their fruit (Matt. 13:24-30).

Notice how thoughts and words grow: like *seeds.* The whole of creation does not respond instantly. Rather, the tiniest of all matter first responds; then the influence grows, becoming visible to the observer. Finally, the results desired and for which one has believed are fully produced.

Remember how we discussed in chapter four that life moves in a direction exactly opposite the forces which cause things to be disorganized? Living things incorporate millions of molecules into their system and organize them into patterns and designs which can be used for energy, building, and reproduction. In similar fashion, the seeds produced by the thoughts and beliefs of people move things in the direction of organization. As a seed grows, so circumstances and events align according to that which is believed. People involved are moved into the right location at the right time. Provisions necessary for the fulfillment of that which is believed somehow make their way into the hands of the believer. Things gradually align and become organized for the fulfillment of that which is believed.

The spiritual world's influence on the natural world is governed by laws comparable to the laws of motion and inertia. For example, there can abide an evilness in things, which can be expelled by the force of good flowing from men and women's hearts. Sometimes great faith, deep commitment, or the joining of many people's hearts is necessary to cleanse certain evil elements which seem resident, or "locked by inertia," within natural things. Once things are cleansed or even moving in a positive direction, that same principle of inertia works in both the spiritual and natural worlds. In other words, once things are redirected in a positive direction, they more easily can be kept in motion. Such forces are real, acting upon both the spiritual and natural world, because the two worlds are integrated.

This gives us a tremendous picture of how the world around us operates. A human being who acts in faith literally, biblically, and scientifically can move a mountain. It may not happen instantly; however, once faith is locked in the heart, quarks move. Quarks and other associated particles influence one another. As one moves, they all begin to move. In time, faith can reorient all particles in association to move according to the faith of a human being. Once those particles of the universe are in motion, the law of inertia will keep them in motion to fulfill that which is believed.

Picture the whole of creation receptive to the thoughts, desires, words, visions, and beliefs of people. Like a womb receives a seed, nurtures it, and allows it to grow, so also creation responds to the seeds coming from people. There is a womb-like quality within creation itself.

Indeed, all of creation came forth from a life-giving God, and using an analogy we can call it "Mother Universe." This is how God created the natural world.*

---

* Recognizing the powerful role man plays in influencing the world does not invalidate the role God can and does play as He sovereignly intervenes in the affairs of men, working miracles independently of man's thoughts, desires and beliefs.

I hope this brings the reader to an understanding of the awesome place mankind holds in the universe and more importantly, to a greater realization of our need to stay intimately connected to the Lord God Almighty. Since our thoughts, visions, and faith both influence the world around us and the generations to follow in such monumental ways, how vital it is that our hearts be centered in Him. Only as our lives are in alignment with His desires and His purposes can we be sure that we are accomplishing and releasing His will in the universe. This awareness calls us to live in constant communion with the Creator.

Conclusion

Science continues to pursue truth but eventually arrives at the spoken Word of God and at God Himself.

When quantum physicists examine the tiniest of all particles, they discover a world which responds to the thoughts of man. As Christians, we know this world was the result of God's thoughts being spoken into existence. The end of discovery then, is the thought and voice of God.

Consider other studies of science which we mentioned.

Scientists observe living creatures, study how animals reproduce, measure how fast plants grow, and even see how living things advance through generations. However, they cannot explain why. Why do things live? Why do they reproduce, grow, and advance? What is this fascinating *push of life*? Where does it originate? The only reasonable answer we have is **God**. On the other side of our most fascinating studies in biology and related fields is His voice: *"Let the earth bring forth...."*

We can talk about laws such as the Second Law of Thermodynamics. Every field of science acknowledges the related force as acting upon all of the universe: chemists can measure how much time it takes for a chemical reaction to move to its lowest state of energy, metallurgists may tell us how long is required for metal to rust away, and astronomers can estimate when a star's nuclear fuel will be exhausted. However, scientifically, no one can explain why this force of increasing entropy exists. Where did it originate? Apart from God, we have no explanation.

We can spend our lives studying certain destructive elements in society. We can examine diseases, war, prejudice, hate, and other consequences of sin. We can see them, but we cannot explain why they exist. Why is there disease? Why is there sin? Why is there suffering? The Bible teaches us that God created mankind. Man has a free will and has, by choice, released these evil forces into the world. They are real. We see them, study them and, to be scientifically truthful, we must say they exist. However, apart from a biblical understanding, we cannot answer the underlying question, "Why?"

There is a force advancing society—a force at the heart of studies in sociology, philosophy, psychology, history.... Obviously, there are many other aspects of mankind that these sciences investigate, but the central underlying feature is a fascination with the force which *moves mankind forward*. We can watch technological advancements, we are aware of new inventions constantly being put before us, and we even can predict that new ideas will come forth in the future. We know that every person is motivated to be active and try to succeed. We can study the advancements of society as a whole and we can see progress throughout history; however, we cannot say where this tremendous power originates or why it exists—apart from God. God *blessed* mankind. He spoke. He released a force which pushes mankind forward.*

Similarly, we see God at the origin of gravity, space, matter, light, and time. Scientists pursue their studies to understand, but the *why* of each one of these stops at the voice of God.

As a student of science, I find the Bible answering each and every question. Unfortunately, many Christians shun the scientific world when they should be standing with our noble scientists helping them put into a biblical perspective the discoveries they have made.

Thousands of scientists have researched, exchanged ideas, investigated, experimented, hypothesized, and theorized, yet they stop where God's voice touches this world. It is no coincidence that the book of Genesis answers the very questions left unanswered by science today. I dare say that the very fundamentals of every field of science lie at the creative voice of God. At His lips we stop.

---

*We also could mention topics related to the nature of man which we discussed in Volumes II through V in this Spiritual Realities series. Without the acceptance of God, who breathed life into man, we cannot explain adequately thought processes, influences between people, paranormal experiences, dreams, experiences through time, how people bond with one another, and other functions of the human spirit which were discussed in earlier volumes.

Yet it also is enlightening to learn that when we stop, we have found Him. To study light is to study His nature. To be amazed at gravity is to behold His omnipotence. To observe man's life and how he relates to others is to investigate the breath of God within us. To think of progress is to see the power of His blessing. To think about time is to ponder His eternal nature. To identify the basic forces which govern this universe is to listen to His spoken Word. In these and all created things, His invisible attributes are evident. In His presence, science stands in awe.

DEVELOPING A PROSPEROUS SOUL
VOL I: HOW TO OVERCOME A POVERTY MIND-SET
VOL II: HOW TO MOVE INTO GOD'S FINANCIAL BLESSINGS

There are fundamental changes you can make in the way you think which will release God's blessings. This is a balanced look at the promises of God with practical steps you can take to move into financial freedom. It is time for Christians to recapture the financial arena.

SPIRITUAL REALITIES

Here they are—the series explaining how the spiritual world and the natural world relate. In this series Harold R. Eberle deals with issues such as:
- What exists in the spiritual world
- Discerning things in the spirit
- Interpretation of dreams
- Angelic and demonic visitations
- Activities of witches, psychics and New Agers
- Spiritual impartations and influences between people
- Science and the Bible including creation, life on other planets, quantum mechanics,...
- Understanding supernatural phenomena from a biblical perspective
- How people access that realm
- Out-of-body experiences
- What the dead are experiencing
- Christian perspective of holistic medicine

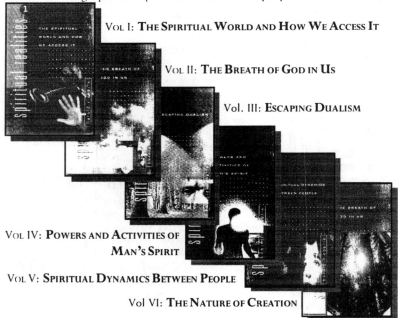

VOL I: THE SPIRITUAL WORLD AND HOW WE ACCESS IT

VOL II: THE BREATH OF GOD IN US

Vol. III: ESCAPING DUALISM

VOL IV: POWERS AND ACTIVITIES OF MAN'S SPIRIT

VOL V: SPIRITUAL DYNAMICS BETWEEN PEOPLE

Vol VI: THE NATURE OF CREATION

PRECIOUS IN HIS SIGHT *A Fresh Look at the Nature of Man*

During the Fourth Century Augustine taught about the nature of man using as his key Scripture a verse in the book of Romans which had been mistranslated. Since that time the Church has embraced a false concept of man which has negatively influenced every area of Christianity. It is time for Christians to come out of darkness! This book, considered by many to be Harold Eberle's greatest work, has implications upon our understanding of sin, salvation, Who God is, evangelism, the world around us and how we can live the daily, victorious lifestyle.

YOU SHALL RECEIVE POWER

Moving Beyond Pentecostal & Charismatic Theology

God's Spirit will fill you in measures beyond what you are experiencing presently. This is not just about Pentecostal or Charismatic blessings. There is something greater. It is for all Christians, and it will build a bridge between those Christians who speak in tongues and those who do not. It is time for the whole Church to take a fresh look at the work of the Holy Spirit in our individual lives. This book will help you. It will challenge you, broaden your perspective, set you rejoicing, fill you with hope, and leave you longing for more of God.

DEAR PASTORS AND TRAVELING MINISTERS,

Here is a manual to help pastors and traveling ministers relate and minister together effectively. Topics are addressed such as ethical concerns, finances, authority, scheduling,.... In addition to dealing with real-life situations, an appendix is included with very practical worksheets to offer traveling ministers and local pastors a means to communicate with each other. Pastors and traveling ministers can make their lives and work much easier by using this simple, yet enlightening, manual.